Instagram Marketing

A Guide to Growing Your Brand with Instagram

Jacob Kirby

© **Rivercat Books LLC Copyright 2022 - All rights reserved.**

The content contained within this book may not be reproduced, duplicated or transmitted without direct written permission from the author or the publisher.

Under no circumstances will any blame or legal responsibility be held against the publisher, or author, for any damages, reparation, or monetary loss due to the information contained within this book, either directly or indirectly.

Legal Notice:
This book is copyright protected. It is only for personal use. You cannot amend, distribute, sell, use, quote or paraphrase any part, or the content within this book, without the consent of the author or publisher.

Disclaimer Notice:
Please note the information contained within this document is for educational and entertainment purposes only. All effort has been executed to present accurate, up to date, reliable, complete information. No warranties of any kind are declared or implied. Readers acknowledge that the author is not engaged in the rendering of legal, financial, medical or professional advice. The content within this book has been derived from various sources. Please consult a licensed professional before attempting any techniques outlined in this book.

By reading this document, the reader agrees that under no circumstances is the author responsible for any losses, direct or indirect, that are incurred as a result of the use of the information contained within this document, including, but not limited to, errors, omissions, or inaccuracies.

Table of Contents

Introduction 1

Chapter 1: Instagram for Business 3

Chapter 2: Types of Instagram Posts 14

Chapter 3: Building a Content Marketing Strategy 26

Chapter 4: Growing a Following 37

Chapter 5: Instagram Analytics 45

Chapter 6: Instagram Advertising 50

Conclusion 55

References 57

Introduction

Social media has grown leaps and bounds in the last ten years, revolutionizing both personal and business communication. Everyone uses social media for various reasons, and it is hard to imagine someone not having a few social media applications or more on their personal devices in this day and age. Out of all the popular ones, Instagram has emerged to be a powerhouse player from the plethora of photo and video sharing applications, and for a long time has been the de facto standard in this category. The application has certainly come a long way since bursting on the scene in 2010. Back then, it was just another social platform allowing you to share pictures of your pets, food, and travels to exotic destinations and even led to the resurgence of the "selfie" trend.

Fast forward to 2022, Instagram has revolutionized itself from just a simple photo-sharing application to a full-stack marketing outlet used by businesses, brands, and influencers. Traditionally, before social media began to take over, the only way a business could begin their online and digital marketing endeavor was through developing and maintaining a domain-hosted website. Whether you had a news outlet, a blog, a product, or a service it was necessary to have a website in order to drive customer traffic for business growth. Nowadays, having a website is a good idea for most businesses, but is far from necessary. Instagram and social media platforms have started to change digital and online marketing as we know it.

With over two billion active users, Instagram is without a doubt the most socially active platform in the world today. According to SendPulse, "the average amount of time spent on the platform by users is 53 minutes every day and at least 90% of users follow at least one company or brand." Whichever industry you belong to, marketing of your services or products on Instagram has never been easier and is certainly a no-brainer. With strategic methods and insightful analytics, a brand can easily scale their business on the platform.

Marketing as a process still needs a lot of effort with understanding of your audience and the platform you're operating on. Thankfully, Instagram makes this simple for the business with their built-in analytics features, which can help in tracking various metrics and KPIs related to customer traffic and engagement. Businesses and brands can also gauge how well their posts are performing based on customer interaction, and hence it is essential for every brand to interact with their followers and nurture them into potential customers. Having the ability to not only direct existing customer traffic to the right channels from the platform, but also growing the audience and attracting new followers through advertising is equally as important. With the right advertising strategy and clickable links, the platform gives every brand and business the opportunity to target the right customers and engage with them through the kind of content they are searching for.

Whether you're a small business owner or social media influencer, this guide will take you through the entire process from setting up your business account to advertising on the platform and will equip you with all the information you need to help you grow and scale your brand with Instagram marketing.

Chapter 1: Instagram for Business

As we continue to grow and make progress in the social media age, it is of paramount importance that businesses and brands continue to evolve, adapt, and welcome all the promotional opportunities that social media platforms can bring. Marketing your products or services on Instagram requires a lot of strategy and consistency with content and engagement with your followers. This section will cover the benefits of marketing on Instagram, creating a business account, and setting your goals.

Creating and maintaining an excellent profile is the first key factor in turning curious visitors into loyal followers who can then interact and engage with the content you create. Content engagement is what begins the process of building that foundational relationship with your followers. Hence why it is imperative for businesses and brands to have an Instagram feed that is just as good as the homepage on their website as more and more people are beginning to look businesses up on Instagram before searching for them on google.

Importance of Having a Business Account

There is a difference between having a classic personal account and a professional business account on Instagram. Initially, if you're a small business, brand, or influencer it is alright to start off with a personal account if you're just putting yourself out there posting decent content on a regular basis. However, as your brand starts to grow and gain more popularity, it can be difficult to keep up with the growth using a personal account. You may not understand what your audience is looking for, you may not post enough content for the Instagram algorithm to promote your profile to more people, etc. This can lead to stagnation in your growth on the platform and it may even decline if the problem is not carefully analyzed. Upgrading to a business account gives you more features that you can use to your advantage to drive a better user experience for your followers. In this section, we will take a close look at how you can easily set up your Instagram profile to be business ready.

While it may be possible to build a brand and market your services or products with a classic personal account if you're an influencer, you have the option to switch to a business profile which will unlock plenty of advanced features like:

- Insight analytics - Analytics will tell you which posts are doing well, how many followers reacted to them, etc.
- Contact and quick reply button - Customers can call or email you directly with the contact button, and quick replies will send pre-written messages to customers for common questions.
- Promoting Posts - Boosting or promoting your posts with advertisements can expand your reach and attract more target audiences.
- Swipe up feature - After crossing 10,000 followers, you can include links in your Instagram stories to redirect traffic to a website, online shop, services, and resources, etc.
- Instagram Shopping - This is a great feature for online retail stores and e-commerce brands, allowing a business account to activate the shop tab which redirects customer traffic to the online store to complete purchasing a service or product.

Setting up Your Business Account

A well-setup business account creates a great first impression, exudes professionalism, and will catch the eye of your potential followers. Popular brands in their respective industries understand the importance of having a seamless profile that makes for a neat and outstanding user experience for their followers.

On the other hand, neglecting a professional setup or not optimizing the user experience on your profile could potentially lead to losing followers to competitors, even if the brand is the leader in the respective industry.

To get started with setting your profile up for business, there are a few ways you can go about getting set up. If you already have a classic personal account and now want to switch to a business account, you can follow these steps:

1. Log in to your Instagram account
2. Select the menu option in the top right corner of your profile
3. Select Settings
4. Select Account
5. Tap "Switch to Professional Account"
6. Tap "Continue"
7. Select from the options of "What best describes you"
8. Select "Business" from the options of "Are you a Creator"?
9. Add your business email, phone number, and address details
10. Tap the button to either display your contact info or select the "Don't use my contact info" to hide your details

11. Tap "Login to Facebook" to connect with your Facebook business page or skip
12. Tap "OK" to complete the switch

If you don't have a personal account on Instagram yet or instead want to make a brand-new account specifically for business, it is highly recommended you set up a Facebook business page first and optimize it for the best user experience. You can also use the following instructions to create a brand-new Facebook business page and link it to your existing Instagram business profile. To create a business page, you can follow these steps:

1. Log in to your Facebook account
2. Select the menu icon in the top right corner beside your profile icon
3. Select "Page" which should direct you to the "Create a Page" screen
4. Add your Page name
5. Select your business Category
6. Add in a brief description about the business
7. Tap "Create Page"
8. Add a profile picture and cover photo
9. Tap "Save"

You can further optimize your Facebook business page by creating a username, adding and removing buttons to direct customer traffic, optimizing for Facebook ads and reviews, adding contact and location details, hours of operations, types of services and price ranges, etc.

It is important to carefully optimize your Facebook business page to create the best user experience for your customers and visitors trying to search you on Facebook. Once you're done setting up your Facebook business page, log in to Instagram through your Facebook details and follow the steps above to set up a business profile on Instagram. Once you have set up your business page and profile on both platforms, you should now be able to consistently post the same content to grow customer engagement on both platforms simultaneously.

Optimizing Account Settings

Now that we've gone over how to properly set up your business profile on Instagram and also briefly went through creating a Facebook business page and linking it to your Instagram business profile, lets now start optimizing your business profile.

Name and Username

It is highly recommended you use your actual business name for the "Name" section to make it easy and recognizable for visitors and existing followers, as this will be your display name right under your profile picture. It is best to keep it simple as there is a 30-character limit, and you want to be cognizant of this if you have a long business name. If you're an influencer, you can use your real name if you're building your brand and creating content focusing on you and your lifestyle.

The username is a unique name to your profile, specific to the platform. You can be creative with this, but generally, it is best to keep it simple, easy to find, and recognizable for visitors and existing followers if they want to engage with you. This is the name that you will use when engaging with your followers and collaborating with other Instagram accounts. Your username should be a reflection of your presence on the platform, so be sure to choose one that resonates with your brand and what you want to be known for.

Profile Picture

Your profile picture should be relevant to your business or brand. So, if you're a small business and already have a logo that defines your brand, you can use that as your profile picture. If you're an influencer and promote a certain type of content around a service or product, you could have a personal picture that resonates with your overall brand vision and message. A good profile picture will leave a lasting image in the minds of your followers, so always have an image that is consistent with your branding. Make sure to leave a little room around the corners of your image, as Instagram will crop your profile picture into a circle.

Bio

Your Instagram bio is like your first introduction to the world, elevator pitch style. This is your opportunity to showcase your personality and let people know who you are and why they should follow you. It should also be concise enough to give potential followers an understanding of the kind of content they can expect from you.

Instagram has a 150-character limit set for your bio, so you want to be as creative and concise as possible.

Your Instagram bio is also the only place where you can feature a clickable link to drive traffic to another website or page. Use a link shortener to shorten the link so that it doesn't take up too many characters, and a link builder if you have more than one link.

If you're an influencer and want to stand out for a specific profession, hobby, skill, or interest, you can describe these details in your bio as well. You can use specific keywords that accurately describe what you do without taking up too much space. Using keywords will not have any effect on your searchability but will put more focus on the kind of content you want your followers to resonate with. You can also include a branded hashtag link to redirect them to another profile that highlights the kind of content your followers might be interested in.

Additional Settings

After you've taken care of the front-end aesthetics of your account, it is also important to optimize a few backend settings to maintain a smooth user experience for your followers. Since you are a public brand or figure, it is important to make sure your account privacy is set to public and not private. This is important as you want people to search you, see your posts and follow you without any obstacles. Once you link your Facebook business page to your Instagram business account, the setting should automatically change to "public account" if you were a private account before, but it is always good to check and see what the privacy setting is when you create your account. To do this, you can go to the menu option of your account > Select Privacy > Select Account > Switch off "Private Account".

Another feature you may want to investigate is hiding offensive comments that could hurt your brand and offend other followers. To do this, you can go to the menu option of your account settings > Select Privacy > Select Comments > Switch on "Hide Offensive Comments".

As your brand grows and you expand your reach to more followers, you may want other people to help you run your social media and Instagram marketing and you can do this by adding up to five more accounts to your business account. To do this you can go to the menu option of your account settings

> Select "Add Account" at the bottom > Enter the username and password of the person you're adding to your business account. This will enable the person helping you to switch between their own account and your business account without having to log in and out of both accounts.

Goals and Objectives

Now that you have your business account set up, let's now go over what exactly you are planning to accomplish with it. Defining goals and objectives for your business account in line with your branding and message is directly proportional to how you market your products or services on the platform.

Use the following questions as a basic framework and try to write down detailed and specific answers so as to define clear goals and objectives:

- What do you want to achieve with your content?
- Is your content going to educate and build awareness with your followers?
- What kind of content and how often are you going to post?
- Who is your target audience and is your current content useful to them?
- How and what are you going to do to keep your audience engaged?
- How do you see yourself progressing every year on the platform?
- What metrics are you interested in tracking to analyze growth?
- How much time and resources can you dedicate to marketing and advertising?

Once you have written down and defined clear goals and objectives, take a look around at your competitors' profiles and gauge what they are doing that maybe you could either adopt or avoid. Study the kind of content they post and how often they post, what are they doing differently to engage with their followers, what do their ads if any look like and how would you advertise differently, etc.

After you've determined what your competitors are doing, take a good hard look at your profile and see how you can stand out from the competition. Analyze your current content and see how you can improve upon it. Maybe you want to archive some old posts containing information that has become outdated and probably needs a repost with more relevant information. Perhaps you want to start posting more frequently. Build a system that helps you continually audit your own account and posts to ensure the quality is up to the mark for your followers.

Benefits of Marketing on Instagram

According to Social Pilot, "Instagram has more than two billion active users and over 64% of users are under the age of 34 years." That's the added advantage of marketing on Instagram. Now that you have a business account and you've defined clear goals and objectives for it, let's understand the benefits and upsides of marketing your products and services on the platform.

Visual Appeal

People are visual beings. If your Instagram profile's feed has great content and a consistent color scheme, visitors are more likely to follow you just based on your ability to provide a soothing visual appeal. People are more willing to engage with visual content that is both concise and informative, which is essential if you want to grab the attention of your followers and visitors as they scroll through endless amounts of content on the platform.

Small Businesses

Instagram has been able to help small businesses with no marketing capital grow their presence simply with consistent content posting. The platform also allows visitors and users to find these small businesses through hashtag links and searches. Even if you don't have a huge marketing budget to advertise your services or products, with a professional setup, posting consistent and relevant content can get the Instagram algorithm working in your favor. Allocating your marketing budget to make your posts look noticeable—in a way that catches the eye of casual visitors—can certainly help grow your audience, especially if you're an influencer.

Brand Awareness

According to SendPulse, "74% of users on the platform consider brands having an Instagram profile or presence on social media as trustworthy and relevant." Users not only admit to learning about new brands and influencers on the platform but also turn away from businesses that do not have a social media footprint. Social media used to be just a nice thing for a business to have, but now, it is a must-have for every business in 2022!

Better Engagement

Having an online presence on social media and especially on Instagram is the best way to build trust and a relationship with your customers. Interestingly, a post on Instagram gets an average of 23% more engagement than it does on Facebook, even though Facebook has more active users. This speaks volumes about how and where your followers would like to engage with you.

Increased Sales

One of the biggest benefits of marketing on Instagram is that the audience tends to make buying decisions a lot quicker than on any other social media platform or website. This certainly does help if you do begin to advertise on Instagram. Fortunately, Instagram helps both brands and businesses with this by making their platform optimized for impulse buying with various tools that take the customer directly from the application to the shop.

Audience Nurturing

Instagram helps you expand your reach by allowing you to accurately identify your target audience. With Instagram ads manager, you can attract the right audience to you based on their demographic information, buying behavior, interests, and other metrics. If a visitor shows interest by clicking on your ads, either they will go through and make a purchase or will be left unsure and decide to come back to it later. In this situation, the ads manager offers strong retargeting alternatives to help encourage the visitor to follow through with their initial interest in your product or service.

Chapter 2: Types of Instagram Posts

You now have a business account, you have set goals and objectives for your growth, and have optimized the account for success. Let's observe in detail the different types of posts that you can make on Instagram and the benefits of each.

Images

Regular images are easily the most common post on the platform for many reasons. You can post a variety of versatile images that increase engagement, pique interest, and escalate curiosity. Getting creative and diverse with image posting is important and should not feel like constant overt advertising to your followers, but rather you want to come off as genuine and real to your followers when posting content with context.

Instagram has a very easy and uncomplicated layout. While the layout hasn't changed much since its inception, there have been enhancements to the platform to compete with other platforms.

The platform still allows you to post photos in landscape and portrait layouts; however, every image post will default to a square image in your profile feed. Evidently, it becomes more important to focus on the quality of your images taking into account resolution, dimensions, and size. You want your audience to be inspired and captivated by your content, so you should always post high-resolution images to your feed.

Since all your images will crop down to a square image in your feed, the standard size for square images is 1080px by 1080px at a 1:1 aspect ratio. For landscape posts the ideal size is 1080px by 566px at a 1.91:1 aspect ratio and for portrait the ideal size is

1080px by 1350px at a 4:5 aspect ratio. Keeping these image proportions in mind, you should always try to edit your images around those dimensions to maintain consistency with your other image posts.

Taking a really good photo can certainly go a long way and this comes with practice and skill. Camera technology has advanced a great deal in the last few years especially with smartphones being able to compete with expensive DSLR cameras. With an awesome phone camera, you too can take spectacular high-quality photos using just your smartphone. Let's explore the following tips to help you take impressive photos that catch the eye of your followers.

Natural Light and Golden Hour

Understanding light is one of the most important aspects of photography. Too much light and your picture looks decolorized and strains the eye, too little and it might create unwanted dark shadows around the light areas of your picture. The best way to counter this problem is to understand light at each part of the day and which areas in your surroundings reflect the best light during those times of the day. Take a few pictures of an object in the same spot, angle, and scene throughout the day to understand the various shades of natural light.

Learn to harness the power of taking pictures during the golden hour of the day. The first hour after sunrise and the first hour before sunset are coveted by photographers and are commonly referred to as the "golden hour." The reason why everyone loves pictures taken during the golden hour is that they have the most aesthetically natural and stunning feel about them. No filters needed!

Rule of Thirds and Space

The rule of thirds is a popular and commonly practiced principle amongst photographers. It is about composition and applies to the arrangement and balancing of all the elements that make up your images like the various shapes, textures, background, colors, and more. A good trick to understand how to use this to enhance the quality of your images would be to utilize the grid line setting in your phone camera and practice learning how to align your images. You divide the frame of your image into three evenly spaced vertical lines and three evenly spaced horizontal lines that will form a 3x3 or nine-part grid. The intersection of the lines is where the focus on your product should take place.

Negative or white is the empty space around your product which is isolated in the frame of the image, this allows you to draw the focus and center the attention on the product. Combining the use of white space and the rule of thirds can really create a powerful high-quality image.

Depth and Layers

We have looked at how using the rule of thirds and spaces can isolate and point the focus solely on the subject; likewise, adding layers and depth to your images can also be naturally interesting. Layering can begin with the focus of one subject, followed by another subject behind it which is slightly blurred, followed by another one in the background which is slightly blurrier again. It is important to not overdo and underdo layering, but experiment with it and test how you can highlight the focus on your main subject while blurring the rest slightly.

Angles and Viewpoints

Have you ever taken a picture with your smartphone or camera and instinctively held it up to around eye level before taking the shot? It is very natural for us to take pictures with this viewpoint but try to mix it up and see how you can take pictures with different viewpoints, maybe a bird's eye view which is high above the ground, or a worm's eye view which is close to the surface of the ground, etc.

Using the gridlines on your camera settings will help point the focus and balance out when taking the pictures from different angles. If you have multiple subjects, try aligning them and experiment with angles and see how well you can portray them in your images vertically, horizontally, and even diagonally if it looks good and the angle makes sense.

Symmetry and Patterns

The human eye is fascinated by a symmetrical composition which enhances a subject that may not be exciting otherwise. Symmetry can help pull the eye into the simple details in the image if it is pleasing to look at. If symmetry is good for the eyes, patterns are good for the brain. Our brains are natural pattern recognition machines and experimenting with patterns can certainly enhance the quality of your images.

Candid, Action, and Detail Shots

Capturing an image with your subjects in motion is a skill on its own but can really make for some amazing shots. It doesn't have to be perfect, even a little movement and a touch of blurriness make for a near artistic image. A great way to get a good stock of candid shots is by first making sure your subject is in good natural light and in the frame of your composition, then hitting the burst mode on your smartphone to capture a bunch of images in a short span of time, and finally when you sift through them you might find one that is "candid" enough to go on your feed.

Vibrant and Humor

Bright colors tend to make us feel warm, happy, and give us energy so sometimes having that burst of bright rich colors can make a big impact on the quality of your images. Finding the right balance of vibrant colors and moderate neutrals can be refreshing to your feed. In the same spirit of adding a little vibrancy, keeping it funny and adding comedy to your images will also add a more real and personal touch that can resonate with your followers.

Editing Images

When you take a look at some really good Instagram profiles and wonder why their image feeds look really good, it's not only because the photos were taken professionally. It's also thanks to the editing process. Editing alone can't make a bad picture look good, so make sure you're following the above steps and are taking high quality photos to begin with. When it comes to editing, there are a plethora of applications and programs that you can use to edit your images. Most of them should have the following editing essentials included.

Crop

Cropping the picture removes any distracting or unnecessary details that you don't want in the final image.

White Balance

White balance helps you adjust the color levels and lighting conditions in your picture if you're not pleased with the original take, and most editing applications will have preset modes you can choose from.

Contrast

Contrast is the range of dark to light tones that help certain elements in your image stand out; too low and you might have a flat image with nothing standing out, or too high you and you will have all tones regardless of the colors standing out, so try to find a balance while avoiding the extremes.

Exposure

Exposure helps you make the picture as bright or dark as you want depending upon the brightness of the original image. Avoid making it too bright or too dark and adjust the exposure moderately.

Saturation

Saturation helps increase the intensity of the colors in your images by making them brighter and adding a dramatic look to your final image. Increased saturation makes your image "pop" with intensity.

Spot clean

Most editing applications should have a spot cleaning feature that can help minimize or remove dusty or gritty elements from the final image, so carefully examine the final image to see if there are any spots you want to reduce or remove.

Filters and Uploading

Once you have completed all the editing on another application of your choosing, it is time to go ahead and upload your final image to your Instagram feed. When you upload an edited picture, it will automatically crop your image into a square if you haven't already done so, and after this, you'll have a few filter options to choose from. If you have edited your image to your liking, you can totally skip adding any additional filters.

You want to always check the final image before posting and write a caption that adds context and meaning behind the image.

Videos

Instagram also lets you post videos. The following tips should help you optimize your videos for marketing success. There is also a plethora of video editing applications that will help you improve the quality of your videos before posting and you want to always be conscious of posting videos that serve a purpose and align with your brand's voice and overall message.

Thumbnail

As with everything else, grabbing your audience's attention even with videos is important, hence you want to be strategic with picking a good thumbnail image that precludes the content in the video. This will help build intrigue and give your followers an idea of what to expect in the video.

Sound

The application tends to auto-play your videos without the sound, so in order for your audience to hear the sound with the video, they would have to tap on it. So, it is a good tip to keep in mind when creating your videos to not rely on the sound as you want your followers to understand the content of your video without having to tap on it. Adding subtitles is a great idea if the video is of someone speaking.

Hyperlapse

Instagram lets you "hyperlapse" your long-form videos or in other words condense the overall length into a shorter one-minute video. Hyperlapse is its own application from Instagram that helps you create effortless and easy time-lapse videos and also lets you choose a playback speed. You can experiment with the length of your videos and see what's comfortable for your audience and what's getting the most engagement.

Boomerangs

Boomerangs are three-second looped videos that play forward and then backward, and these can be fun and entertaining for your audience and can be anything like some fun moments behind the scenes or some celebratory toasting of wine glasses etc.

Instagram Reels

In order to keep up with the competition from other applications with short-form video content, the platform's newest feature called Instagram Reels allows you to create entertaining video clips ranging from 15—30 seconds for just about any purpose, such as information videos and quick tutorials. They have their own section on the platform so when creating content to market your product, taking advantage of Reels is a great opportunity to increase traction and engagement with your followers. At least 100 million reels get watched every day! The following steps should help you with posting Instagram Reels:

1. Tap the plus icon on the top of your screen and select Reel
2. Accordingly, adjust your settings:
    - Timing - choose if it's a 15 or 30 second Reel
    - Music - type in the search bar for the music you want to use
    - Speed - choose if you want to speed up or slow down the pace
    - Effects - select any applicable effects if you need to
    - Timer - set a timer or a countdown before the reel begins recording
3. Record your Reel and accordingly pause or resume recording if you need to switch to a new scene by keeping an eye on the progress bar at the top of the screen.
4. Review the recording and re-edit if you're not satisfied. If you are satisfied, then hit the "Share To" icon on the bottom right of the screen to either share to Reels or to Stories.

Sharing the clip to Reels will automatically appear on the separate Instagram Reels page and you will also have the option to share it to your feed amongst other additional settings like tagging other people or cropping the display image of the Reel. If you're not ready to post it yet, you can choose to save it to your draft to post later as well.

When you select the Stories option, you can either share it to your Instagram stories or with close friends only.

Instagram Stories

Instagram stories are another feature where you can post a lot more real and authentic images and videos that aren't as polished as your profile feed. These posts last for just 24 hours, after which they disappear. Unlike with your main feed, you can experiment with Stories and bring about a real and genuine side to your brand or business where you can post some less-polished content. This is a great place to share behind the scenes of your business. Instagram Stories are also a great way for businesses to be discovered when paired with the search capabilities of the platform. Here's how you start post to your Instagram Stories:

1. Tap the plus icon on the top of your screen and select "Story"
2. Select the photo or video you would like to upload
3. Add any extra features like location, text, filters, poll, music, etc.
4. Tap the "Send To" button and publish your story

Another great feature of the platform is that Instagram lets you save the best and finest stories as Instagram Highlights from your Instagram Stories. Images and videos cannot be directly added to highlights and they would need to be posted as Stories first. Instagram Highlights are a great way to add more detail about your brand or business that you want to segregate from your bio and main feed, like your working hours, testimonials, or various services. They normally appear right under your bio and are a great way to make temporary content permanent. There are two ways to add stories to highlights—from current stories or from your archive.

Here's how you can add current stories to highlights:

1. Open a published or current story and click on the heart icon at the bottom of your screen.
2. Add the story to an existing Highlight or create a new one if you don't have any yet.
3. Once the story has been posted to the highlight, you can then edit the cover image or pick a new name for the highlight.

Here's how you can add stories from your archive to highlights:

1. Access your archive on the top right of your profile. The archive will contain stories that expired after their 24-hour limit and any other posts that you removed in the past.
2. Select the story and then click on highlight at the bottom of the menu and select which highlight you want to add it to.

Instagram Live

While Stories are a great way to showcase curated pre-recorded content with an expiration date, Instagram Live is another feature that lets you engage with your audience in real time. It may be intimidating for many growing, up-and-coming brands to venture into the live space. It always helps to prepare in advance and have an agenda if you plan on using Instagram Live. Live is a great way to engage with your audience in real-time through discussions and Q&A.

When you go live on Instagram, you have the option to broadcast it to your Instagram Stories to let current users on the platform know you're live and even send a notification to offline users to come hang out. You can invite guests to your livestreams for collaborations which opens the door to plenty of other marketing possibilities!

Chapter 3: Building a Content Marketing Strategy

Every online business needs a strong tactical marketing channel with a well-thought-out strategy. Developing a marketing strategy shouldn't be complicated, but attention to detail, patience, and consistency will certainly see a significant return on investment with time. This section will outline everything you need to consider when developing your marketing strategy on Instagram.

Setting Goals

When developing any business or marketing strategy, it is no surprise setting goals is always the first task that needs to be undertaken. Setting your goal for marketing on Instagram should always begin with asking yourself why you are on the platform and what are you looking to achieve from promoting your business or brand on it. There are plenty of reasons and they can be as follows:

- You could already be an established brand or business and want to attract more followers from varied demographics.
- You are looking to grow brand awareness and increase your reputation in your industry.
- You perhaps want to gain more insights into a market and audience while testing a new venture or idea.
- You could be looking to build a community with your followers and provide knowledge on certain products and services that aren't satisfied elsewhere.

- You probably want to boost sales and increase revenue with promotional campaigns.

No matter what goals you define to build the overall framework for your marketing strategy, it is important to always align them with the SMART strategy: Specific, Measurable, Attainable, Relevant, and Timely.

Defining Your Target Audience

Determining your target audience is a crucial step in setting your marketing strategy up for success. Simply put, you want to be growing your audience with people who are genuinely interested in your products or services as there is a higher chance of engagement from them. Catering to the wrong audience will undermine your marketing strategy drastically.

One of the standard ways to avoid this is to craft a buyer persona or avatar and understand their demographics and interests. Utilize data-driven methods to first gain insights into your audience and learn about their—age, gender, location, occupation, earning capacity, and more. The more specific and detailed you can get, the better understanding you will have of them.

Another way is to search for hashtags related to your business, brand, market, or industry and look for the profiles engaging with these hashtags to learn about their behavior, pain points, concerns, and desires.

Analyzing Competitors

Analyzing what your competitors are doing is a wise move. It's always better to understand the overall playing field in the market and find opportunities where you can stand out from the competition. If you know who the top competitors in your industry or market are, you can look up their profiles and note down details regarding their content, engagement, growth, and other metrics. Repeat this process until you have enough data gathered from at least the top five or top ten profiles and then start to analyze all the collected data for commonalities and patterns. Once you're done with your analysis, you should have a good idea what kind of content your competitors are posting, and which posts get the most engagement. It's a good idea to also review their comment sections for any feedback their customers are providing. This is a great way to gauge what customers are both happy and dissatisfied about. With this information, you can identify missed opportunities and loopholes that you could take advantage of.

Designing Quality Content

We have looked at the various types of content that you can post on Instagram in earlier chapters, and it goes without saying as a brand or a business you want your content to look both appealing and pleasing to the eye. Content is certainly king on every social media platform and quality content is what separates the best profile from the average one. Your content might be centered around the promotion of your products and services, motivational posts, brand or company culture. But if the content is not up to the mark, your followers might switch over to your competitors who might be putting out better quality content. Hence investing in designing quality content is critical to marketing success on the platform.

Consistent Aesthetic

Having a disorganized flow of aesthetics around your content could not only cause your marketing to fall flat but also you may lose followers. Whether you attract new followers or retain your existing following, it is important to understand that in the minds of the audience on a visual platform they recognize you and mentally segregate you from everyone else's content.

Following your brand aesthetic with consistency is very important. The visuals your profile and feed exude should align with your brand personality. Consistently maintaining a theme or a visual concept across all your social media platforms including Instagram will certainly help with establishing yourself as a brand in the eyes of your followers.

Outline an Editorial Calendar

It is no secret that growing on any social media platform requires consistent content delivery. On average, the most successful brands post some form of content at least twice a day. Now as a new brand or business just beginning their foray into the world of online and digital marketing, this may or may not feel like a monumental responsibility in the beginning but will eventually hit a stumbling block. You might run out of ideas, feel burnt out, or lose consistency.

The easiest way to stay efficient and consistent is by creating a scheduling calendar that will outline your content delivery over a certain period of time. There are plenty of tools and applications that can help you plan your posting times in advance along with the content, captions, and hashtags. You can also use these tools to automate the posting and gain analytical insights for more information about your posts.

Converting Your Followers into Customers

We should not forget at the end of the day the overall goal for marketing on Instagram is to grow your brand or business by leading your customers from the platform to purchase your products or services. The engagement on the platform alone isn't enough to boost revenue, hence while running promotional campaigns, always try to include a call to action (CTA) in your captions by instructing your followers to click the link in your bio, as your bio is the only place where you can include links.

Implementing Your Content Strategy

Now that you understand the importance of building a content marketing strategy on the platform, let us now look at how we can put the plan into action. We've already gone over the various types of posts there are at your disposal to use on the platform in the form of images, videos, stories, and live. This section should give you an idea of the methods and variations of those posts that you can use in your marketing strategy.

Images

There are many different variations of image posts that you can use in your strategy, and you might even come up with your own variations, so always be creative and don't be afraid to test or experiment with new ideas. It is also important for these posts to come off as real and authentic and not staged in any manner that may make your audience feel you are advertising heavily for a call to action.

Behind-The-Scenes Posts

These posts are a great way to give your audience a view behind the curtains of just about any occasion, event, or work that you might be doing.

Educational Posts

These posts have a great track record of doing well, especially if your audience are following you for guidance on certain topics that they are less knowledgeable about. These types of posts help you to establish yourself as an authority.

Influencer Posts

Working with a social media influencer who has a large following by promoting and speaking about your product or service is a great way of opening up your brand and business to an untapped audience.

Motivational Posts

Motivational posts are a great way to amplify your brand's message and values to your audience, depending on what kind of business or brand you are running.

User-Generated Content (UGC)

While it is important to focus on creating original content for your audience, there is so much that can also be gained from user-generated content or content that your followers tag you in or post with your brand hashtag. As long as the post aligns with your message and credit is given to the person, this is a great way to feature your own audience on the platform and even show that you truly care about them.

Holiday Posts

There is almost a holiday for every occasion and event around the world and as your brand grows online and reaches many across the globe, taking part or celebrating the holiday with a post can not only be a great way of strengthening your bond with your audience who will appreciate you for it but also reach out to more potential followers in that demographic.

Shopping Posts

These posts are definitely your best odds for driving sales and increasing revenue as long as they are posted in moderation and not constantly advertised. Shopping posts should have your products or services tagged in the post which makes it easy for your followers to tap on the info box which will redirect them to your shop and help them complete their purchase.

Carousel Posts

With Carousel posts, you can post up to 10 images or videos in a single carousel post and in the same format. They are a creative way to promote new products or services and you can be really creative with them by providing more context about the product or service, customer testimonials, before and after sequences, and any events you organized for the product or service.

Videos

We have already established video content tends to get more traction than image posts, so including high-quality and well-edited videos should be part of your marketing strategy since there is really no limit to what can be done with one-minute Instagram videos. According to HubSpot, 64% of consumers are more likely to purchase a product after watching a video of it first. So, it is very important to keep the following pointers in mind when creating compelling video content.

Promote Your Products

As you begin to create your video message, promoting your product the right way is important for you to stand out from the competition without pushing bland videos with no message to the market. Always focus on leading with value and let your audience know how the product is going to benefit them first.

Educate Your Audience

Depending upon your products or services, you may want to educate the audience on what exactly the product or service provides, and why that may benefit them.

Build Trust with Your Followers

As always, it is important to establish trust with your followers. Making sure that you communicate your video message in line with the culture and values that your brand has advocated for will always be admired and looked up to by your audience.

Instagram Stories

As we mentioned earlier, Stories are a great way to engage with your audience and pull in new followers. Businesses and brands are starting to see the value of posting short-form content, which doesn't have to be completely professional. We'll dive into some of the best ways to use Stories below.

How Often to Post Stories?

This is extremely important when you start to build out your marketing strategy. Stories are time-consuming, and you as the brand or business will need to decide how often you would like to post to your stories. Post too much and your followers might stop paying attention. Posting less might either give way for your competitors to overtake you or you might lose followers as there is a lack of engagement. Finding the optimal middle ground for your business that aligns with your brand and message is key because what may work for someone else might not necessarily work for you. Basically, test out what suits you and what gets the highest level of engagement from your particular audience!

When to Post Stories?

With regular posts, it is important to be posting when your followers are at their peak engagement time. However, for stories, since they have a 24-hour window unless you add them to highlights, you have the flexibility to post at any time of the day without issue!

What Stories to Post?

The platform has really made it easy and has plenty of creative tools that you can use to put out great stories. As we have discussed earlier, it doesn't have to be all professional and business-like; you can bring about a fun and comical side to your brand or business. Analyzing the stories which have more engagement should tell you all you need to know about the kind of content your followers like to engage with.

Instagram Stories Features

Here are some features that you can play around with when posting Instagram Stories that will not only help increase comments from your existing following but may also get casual visitors interested as they tap on your profile picture.

Location

Ever since the platform introduced stickers, they have become a great means of engagement and can be quite fun to play around with. A great example would be if you are in a restaurant and tag that restaurant's location with a sticker, you will appear in that location's stories, and this is a fun way to drive visitors from both profiles to each other.

Hashtags

The same goes with hashtag stickers too, if you post a story and add that hashtag as a sticker, it will appear on the hashtag's page, and any casual visitors on the hashtag page can then come and view your profile if they are interested in your content.

Links

This is a big deal for all brands, businesses, and influencers, as Stories is the only place where you can add clickable links other than the bio, and a bonus would be if you save that story as a highlight for future reference for your audience. Having the ability to drive traffic from your Instagram profile to external links is critical for your marketing on the platform.

Collaborations

As you work and collaborate with other profiles and influencers, tagging them would be a great way to drive engagement and gain more followers as all parties leverage each other's followings.

Polls, Questions, and Sliders

This is another great feature for brands and businesses as this is a direct opportunity to engage with the audience by surveying them about ideas, your products, services, and more. You can even be quite direct with this feature and directly poll your audience about what kinds of content they prefer.

Countdown

This is a great feature to implement, especially when you want to hype your audience up for a sale or launch or just about anything after a countdown.

Gifts and Memes

These will never age, and it is always fun to add an expressive comical personality to your brand. Even better that Instagram allows you to find and add them from a library easily as well.

Instagram Live

Instagram Live is a great way to have your audience engage with you, and you should definitely be using this feature as part of your overall marketing strategy.

Tease Something

Recently, plenty of brands and businesses are using Live to tease or talk about a new product launch, service, or event. This is a great way to build hype and get your audience intrigued about what you're about to launch or drop. Obviously, you don't want to give away all the details so teasing about what you're about to do and setting expectations on the date and time is a great way to drive results positively.

Q&A, Tutorials, and Workshops

This is another great way to engage with your audience, especially if you're someone they come to for help and advice.

Promote Your Campaigns

Promoting your campaign is a great way to use the Live feature and you can even get creative with it while driving a sense of urgency with your followers. Dropping discount codes and one-time promotional offers for the followers on Live with you can boost your viewership and engagement massively.

Chapter 4: Growing a Following

In the previous chapters, you have read about the importance of Instagram marketing, the various types of posts, and how to build a content strategy with them. In this section, we will look at optimizing your content strategy to grow your following. Your Instagram profile is more than just your following, it is your online community. Purchasing followers is never a good option as you will never get any engagement from them, nor will your content be of any value to them. Your resources should always be spent building your following and nurturing them to become long-time customers. The only way to grow an organic following is by creating high-quality compelling content and optimizing that content to reach as many new followers as possible. This section will go into detail about some very useful ways to organically grow your audience without purchasing them or using spam bots.

Profile Curation

The reason why curating your profile is important, is because humans are visual beings first. Creating a good first impression for your visitors is important if you want them to follow you. Maintaining a consistent color aesthetic and theme for your profile that resonates with your overall brand can enhance the visual appeal and vibe of your profile, giving off a professional feel and look.

Use Reels

You have read and understood what reels are about, their importance, and how prominent they are in today's marketing strategy. Tapping into the power of reels can really help grow your audience if done right because reels are right now by far the most highly engaging type of content on Instagram. You may feel like using reels won't make sense with your brand or business's overall marketing strategy, but creativity has no bounds. Your followers will always appreciate you for your originality and if you put effort into creating high-quality content for them.

Optimize Your Captions

This is a really big tip or "hack" for anyone looking to grow their following: Optimizing your post captions for search or in other words, search engine optimization (SEO). Search engine optimization is a strategy in and of its own, and implementing a strategy that optimizes all your posts is the easiest way to get more casual visitors to your profile. The platform itself is a giant search engine of its own and uses machine learning to find high-quality content that is relevant to you based on your search criteria. This is important as many users on the platform find content by typing keywords into the search bar, giving them a plethora of options from hashtags to profiles to look at. There are plenty of factors behind the algorithm that make up the criteria for curating the best content and while having the right keywords is important, it is equally essential to have high-quality posts with well-written captions as well.

Hashtag Strategies

Investing in a hashtag strategy is another great tip and "hack" that if implemented the right way will yield a significantly high ROI. According to SocialPilot, "Posts with at least one hashtag get 12% more engagement and on average every post contains at least ten hashtags." Using the right and relevant hashtags that make sense and align with the overall message of your post is critical, as this will bring in more followers who utilize the search feature.

There are plenty of popular hashtags that might seem saturated and congested with too many irrelevant posts. To counter this, it is always important to analyze the hashtags your audience, competitors, and industry leaders use that have a huge level of engagement. This is where you can niche down with hashtags and target more specific, less competitive hashtags.

Giveaways

Who doesn't love giveaways? Giveaways are a great marketing tactic to grow your audience, and if done right and with the right strategy, you have the potential to attract many more followers. Setting clear expectations and entry criteria is crucial here and there are plenty of options like posting to stories or tagging a friend that can expand your reach.

Influencers and Brands

Partnering with influencers and brands to engage their audiences to promote your products or services is a great marketing strategy and can benefit all parties involved. According to SendPulse, "brands tend to gain five times more ROI from the amount spent on influencer marketing and brand partnerships." That is what makes this marketing strategy a no-brainer. However, making sure you work with the right influencer and brand is essential. You want to be able to work with an influencer who resonates with your product or service, so it makes it easier for them to promote you on their social media platforms to gain attention and attract their followers to you. Similarly, when working with a brand, you want to find ways how your product or service pairs well with theirs. You should always do a quick background review of the influencer or brand you want to work with to gauge how they are interacting with their audiences and how much engagement you can expect from them. Determining whether their engagement is genuine, authentic, and aren't bots is another important element of this strategy.

Guest Takeovers

This is an untapped and unorthodox marketing trick that if done right can certainly grow your following. Featuring a guest—an employee, an influencer, a celebrity, or just someone other than yourself behind the brand that everyone is used to seeing every day can be a great way to hook your audience and followers' interest. You can promote in advance that your guest will take over the stories in a Q&A or AMA (Ask me Anything) format.

Shareable Content

You have read about how important it is to create high-quality content in the previous chapters and the reason why that has been stressed is that it does a lot for your marketing in terms of shareability. Not only does creating high-quality content inspire your audience and can drive them to a call to action, but it can also encourage them to share it with their own followers. The content doesn't have to be all serious, sometimes even a meme or a gif that aligns with your brand might be a bit of fun and could be huge if it is already trending in pop culture. The more your fun non-business posts resonate with your audience the more likely they are to share your content.

Inbound Interaction

Another great tip to increase engagement with your following is to have them interact with you through AMA's and Q&A's, which you can respond to in a stream of Instagram Stories. This is extremely helpful if you are a subject matter expert on something and can offer advice and knowledge to your followers who can also share that with people they know, in turn bringing more visitors to your page. This process of inbound interaction is a great way to establish trust and not only helps grow your audience but also their interest and loyalty to your brand and business. Another great tip with inbound interaction is taking the time to respond and react to all the comments you receive on your posts from your followers, especially if it is feedback or any thoughts and ideas that they have for you.

Value Proposition

Having an outline of expectations on what your customers are going to get from following you is important. Picture walking into a restaurant or a food chain and not knowing what type of food they make. That probably won't be the best experience, and you would likely turn around and go to a place you know what to expect from. Your profile and brand follow the exact same principles. A clear value proposition of the kind of content you have created is critical in turning visitors into followers and eventually customers.

Cross-Promotion

While marketing on Instagram, it is also important to note that the platform is only one marketing channel and as a business, you should leverage as many highly engaging social platforms as possible like TikTok, Facebook, and YouTube. You also have an option to link your Facebook business page as we discussed in an earlier chapter.

Challenges

One of the most popular social media challenges that went viral, and nearly everyone knows about it is the ice bucket challenge from 2014. Social media challenges have recently seen a surge and are a great way to grow an audience and create new trends. This is also a great way to engage with your followers and has the potential to reach millions of users by having them take the challenge and tagging you with a branded hashtag. Keep the challenges simple and easy to do, and always appreciate your audiences for taking the time to engage with you through them.

UGC

Speaking of appreciating your audiences, one of the best ways to do so is by using the content generated through branded hashtags, or in other words—user-generated content. There are many ways you can utilize user-generated content in addition to your strategy of creating original content. You could run a challenge and have your followers tag you with the challenge in the branded hashtag, and when you sift through the content, you could add a carousel post of the top five submissions, as an example. This is a great way to feature your audience on the main feed of your profile and could motivate the rest of the audience to want to participate again the next time. This is a great way to build a bond with your community and increase engagement organically.

Accessibility

Making your content accessible to everyone is extremely important and will certainly go a long way to show you care about all your followers. It is simple things like adding subtitles or text overlays, capitalizing all the words appropriately in your captions, ensuring great sound quality for your audio and video posts, and describing visuals in detail if possible are some great ways to make your content both accessible and inclusive for some of your audience who are hard of hearing or have vision impairment.

Consistency

With any type of social media marketing, content is king and consistency is key. You have already read through how important it is to post high-quality content consistently. There are plenty of ways to keep your content marketing strategy on Instagram running on all four wheels. Some of them are investing in scheduling applications and tools; you will find many of them on the internet so always do your research and weigh out the differences between free and paid and always go with the option that gives you the most benefits that reduce your time. You could also hire a virtual assistant or a social media marketing manager to keep a tight schedule with posting on your account by following the steps mentioned in earlier chapters by linking their accounts with your business profile.

Another pro tip is to analyze your audience's high activity and engagement times throughout the week on each day to gain insights into what are the best times to post on the platform. You want to be able to maximize your ability to reach more followers and casual visitors during high activity times to have a better chance at growing your followers.

Chapter 5: Instagram Analytics

As you bring all the elements of your marketing strategy together and start to implement it, you will come to realize the need to understand if your strategy is yielding any results. Any marketing strategy after a certain duration will require some form of data analysis to understand how well it is performing. The best advantage of upgrading your profile to a business account is that you get access to Insights which is a tool used for such analytics.

Analytics is the best way to gain insights about what kind of content your audience enjoys engaging with and when they are most active during the day. It is important to know this information in order to set your marketing strategy up for success. Picking the right metrics to track is important as there is a plethora of them, and you will most likely want to track metrics that are curated specifically for your marketing strategy. As every business and brand is different, their marketing strategy and analytics will equally be different from each other.

In this chapter, you will understand all you need to know about Instagram analytics and growing your account, improving your marketing strategy, and reaching target audiences. We will also view the importance of audience growth and various post analytics based on the metrics each post comes with.

Instagram Audience Analytics

No matter what metrics your marketing strategy is designed around, you must always be analyzing and studying data about your audience because after all, every social media marketing strategy requires you to grow an audience, nurture new followers, and convert them into future customers. Some key audience metrics that you must always consider are the following:

- **Location** - You will want to know which part of the world, country, and city most of your followers are located to help you determine what might be the best time to post according to their time zone and during their most active times.
- **Age** - You will also want to analyze and see which age group resonates with your content to accordingly decide the frequency of your posting times as more younger followers tend to spend more time on social media.
- **Gender** - An important demographic metric in determining which gender resonates more with your content, and this should accordingly help you curate more content specifically for them.

Another key metric you want to pay attention to is the followed and unfollowed metrics that will tell you how many followers you lose and gain every day. Obviously, you want to minimize the unfollowed and increase your followed metrics. So, keep an eye on this metric as you consistently post on your profile, and note any irregular spikes which could tell you if the content was either well received or not.

Feed Post Analytics

We have talked about the importance of building your main feed and using a strategic mix of both video and image content. As you continue to put out quality content on your main feed, it becomes essential to analyze over time to determine how well your posts are doing. That will give you an idea if your content fits well with the Instagram algorithm and if it is helping your content reach more eyes. Important performance metrics to track are likes, comments, shares, saves, and clicks. Analyzing these metrics should give you a good understanding of the number of interactions that have taken place on that post and how many accounts did the content reach. You can even encourage your followers to save and share your content if they find it helpful. This is a great tip, especially if it is video content, as this will continually build passive engagement over time as your followers keep coming back to view the post. Encouraging your followers to share your content with someone they might know is also a great way to attract new like-minded followers and build a strong community.

Stories Analytics

You read about Instagram Stories earlier in chapter two and also discovered how easy-going you can be with the various types of posts you can share to Stories. Instagram helps you track if your Stories content was well received by your audience or not with the following metrics:

- Back
- Forward
- Excited
- Next Story
- Link clicks
- Impressions
- Profile Visits
- Text button taps
- Swipe ups

Reviewing each of these metrics can tell you how your audience navigated your stories: If they clicked on any links or text boxes you added in, if they reacted to your story, and if they visited your profile from the story. Some other key metrics that you can track are the watch-through rate and completion rate per story. The watch-through rate calculates the percentage of viewers who watched your stories from the beginning to end and the completion rate calculates the percentage of viewers who watched the complete length of each slide in your stories. Analyzing these two metrics along with the others can give you a clear picture of what is working and what you can improve on based on the content you post to stories.

Reels and Live Analytics

We have gone through the importance of using Instagram Reels and Live and have also read about how crucial they are to your content marketing strategy. Some key metrics you will see for both live and reels are how many times they were played, the number of interactions on the reel post, the number of accounts the reel reached, and other engagement metrics like comments, saves and likes. Reels is currently the best post on the platform and taking advantage of it can help you increase your reach. With Instagram Live, you will see comments, reactions, and the total number of viewers who were present during the Live, amongst other metrics. This is really helpful information to have for when you plan to host more Lives in the future.

Shopping Analytics

We reviewed earlier how you can optimize your account to integrate your online store and also looked at how you can create shopping posts with external links tagged in the post. Another feature you will want to enable is Instagram Checkout.

At the end of the day, your marketing strategy should drive your followers to want to take action when they view your shopping posts, and it is important to keep an eye on the posts that drive the most value for your brand. Two key metrics that shopping analytics can help you track are product page views and product button clicks. If your product page has high page views but low button clicks, this could be an indicator that either the price of the product is high, or the product description isn't compelling enough.

Chapter 6: Instagram Advertising

The final part of this book is about Instagram advertising and reviewing if advertising on the platform makes sense for your brand and business or not. There are a lot of benefits to advertising on Instagram in terms of exposure to a targeted audience, generating leads for your business, and the opportunity to drive traffic to an external site. Running advertisements is a big decision you will make as a business or brand owner, so it is always best to do some homework and ask yourself if you are ready to run ads and what are you looking to achieve by running ads.

It normally makes sense to run ads when your business is just starting to take off as the advertisements are simply a method of amplifying the effort you have taken to organically grow your business or brand up until this point. You don't want to spend money running ads when they won't convert, nor do you want to run poor-quality ads that don't have a desirable call to action. It is also important to understand the mindset you must go in with when you are beginning to advertise on the platform and that unless it is a brilliant stroke of luck, not all of your ads will perform well or convert. Also, your ads may at some point start to decline in performance. All of these concerns are part of the process and should not discourage you from analyzing what went wrong and trying to get a winning formula again.

Once you have made up your mind and have decided you want to take the plunge with advertising, this section will give you all the information you need to set up and run your first of many ad campaigns.

You have read about linking your Instagram business profile to a Facebook Business page in the first chapter of this book, and this is extremely important as Instagram uses Facebook's advertising platform to run ads. If you made a Facebook page in the beginning when you started your marketing journey on Instagram, the following strategies should be easy to implement as all the setup, budgeting, scheduling, creating, and running of the ad will be done through Facebook itself.

Research

Research is always important before you venture into something new, and you have read through this book about how researching your competitors is important. Spending time researching what your competitors and the industry leaders are doing will help you understand their calls to action, their engagement levels, and the types of ads that are converting.

There are two ways to research the ads your competitors run. The first method is by referring to their Facebook business page and clicking "Page Transparency" to see the history of all the ads they ran linked with Instagram and other platforms as well. Generally, if the ad is still up, there is a good chance it is doing well.

The second method of research is a little experimental, especially if they are using a remarketing strategy. Start by viewing their profile on Instagram and then click their website link in their bio. When you get redirected to their website, browse through a few of their products and click on a few to read their product descriptions. Exit and log back into Instagram, and when you return back on the platform you might see their retargeting ad on your home feed.

Objectives

Campaign objectives are basically what you need visitors and followers to do when they see your ads. For advertising on Instagram, the campaign objectives are a little different compared to Facebook campaign objectives, and they are as follows:

- **Brand awareness** - You want to reach more people and create awareness about your brand and business.
- **Reach** - You want to get your ad out to as many viewers as possible.
- **Traffic** - You want to drive the click-through rate to external websites and stores.
- **App installs** - You want to send people to your online store to make a purchase.
- **Engagement** - You want to drive engagement on your posts through likes, comments, shares, and saves.
- **Conversions** - You want visitors to make certain decisions, like signing up to an email list, or completing a purchase.

One important note to mention is if your objective is to sell online products or services and you want to run a remarketing campaign, you must install a Facebook pixel, which is a small piece of code that you can place on your website to track visitors.

Targeting

Targeting is trying to find the right people to advertise to who are most likely to take action and follow through with a purchase. Instagram has the same targeting options as

Facebook which include location, demographics, and behavior, among other options.

At the basic level, you want to select the location, age, gender, and language to start with. You also have the option to create a Custom Audience, or a Lookalike Audience based on both platform setups. From here you have two options to narrow your criteria even further with either Facebook Audience Insights or Google Analytics.

Creative

Designing your ad creatives for Instagram is both an art and science with the purpose of reaching the right people and motivating them with the right tone to engage with your ad. Instagram has four types of ads you can choose from:

- Carousel - These are great options to showcase multiple products or multiple uses of a single product.
- Single Image - Images are simple if you are getting started with advertising on the platform and are quite easy to set up and perform very well.
- Single Video - Videos are the best for hooking your audience with 30–60 second clips and definitely have the best return on investment.
- Slideshow - These are great if you have limited resources and can simply put together a video with still images like a presentation.

Once you have set your objectives, determined your target audience, and designed your creatives, it is now time to create your first ad with the following steps:

1. If you have your Instagram business profile linked to your Facebook business page, click on Instagram Ads and enter your credentials.
2. Head over to Facebook Ads Manager and click on the " + Create" button on the top left of your screen.
3. Enter your campaign objectives and create a pixel if you are choosing to do retargeting.
4. Create your Ad Set by choosing the audience preferences and your budget spend.
5. Click continue to choose the type of ad you want to run and add your text caption and headline for the ad.
6. Preview your ad to see how it will look before you run it and make any changes if needed.
7. Check other distribution options if you want to run it on Facebook as well.
8. If everything looks good, click Confirm.

Tracking

Now that you have successfully set up and launched your ad campaign, as with anything else it is important to track and measure the performance in order to edit and optimize it for success. You should be able to see the performance metrics of your Instagram ad on the Ads manager after you place your order. You can also use Ads manager to customize and play around with the features to show you results based on your objectives. If the ad is performing well for the first few days, you can then increase the ad spend every three or four days and keep tracking the performance. If the ad stops performing or starts to decline, you can then shut it off to analyze where it stopped performing and then start a new one again.

Conclusion

You now have all the important information at your disposal in this book to guide you in building a strong Instagram marketing strategy. New strategies are constantly emerging as the platform evolves, but this book should give you a good base to start with. Understand that marketing and growing your following will not yield results overnight, and this is a long-term game plan that you should be prepared for. At no point should you take the easy route and resort to shortcuts by purchasing followers, as they won't engage with your content and more than likely will be bots that spam messages and harass your organic following.

Take your time and experiment with the content, see what works and keep up with the trends in pop culture to try to weave them in with your content strategy if possible. Focus on crafting simple goals and targets with your marketing strategy, and always leverage other platforms to drive and pull traffic appropriately. Depending upon your marketing budget you can either invest in external tools, software, applications, and people to help you with your marketing and advertising on the platform to save time, or if you are patient and not in a hurry, you can organically grow your following with consistent posting and engagement.

Utilize all the types of Instagram posts at your disposal to the best of your abilities and always go for quality over quantity. Remember that content is king, and quality is key when crafting your marketing strategy for Instagram to grow an organic following.

When you finally choose to run Instagram ads, always research your competitors first and choose the right objectives. Also, be sure to create and install a Facebook pixel if you intend to run a remarketing campaign. Finally, always start with a small ad spend with gradual increase if the ad performs well, making tweaks to your ad as necessary along the way.

I hope you have enjoyed learning about marketing on Instagram, and I wish you the best of luck in your endeavors!

References

Allie Decker. (2017, April). *Instagram marketing: The ultimate guide.* Hubspot.com. https://www.hubspot.com/instagram-marketing

Bagadiya, J. (2021, December 14). *50+ Instagram statistics you should know in 2022.* SocialPilot. https://www.socialpilot.co/instagram-marketing/instagram-stats

Chacon, B. (2017, November 24). *Instagram ads: A step-by-step guide to running your own ad campaign.* Later.com. https://later.com/blog/instagram-ads/#ARTICLE_SECTION_0

Chen, J. (2019, September 4). *How to take good Instagram photos: 5 tips to try now.* Sprout Social. https://sproutsocial.com/insights/how-to-take-good-instagram-photos/

Cyca, M. (2018, September 12). *How to take good Instagram photos: A step-by-step guide.* Social Media Marketing & Management Dashboard. https://blog.hootsuite.com/how-to-take-good-instagram-photos/

Holmes, J. (2015). *Instagram black book: Everything you need to know about Instagram for business and personal* - ultimate Instagram marketing book. Lexington, Kentucky.

Later. (2022). *Instagram marketing: The definitive guide (2022 Update).* Later.com. https://later.com/instagram-marketing/#chapter1

Medical, B. (2020, February 3). *Instagram business vs. personal accounts: 4 benefits you should know.* Boost Medical. https://boostmedical.com/instagram-business-vs-personal/

Molendijk Media. (2022, May 21). *How to create a Facebook business page 2022.* Www.youtube.com. https://www.youtube.com/watch?v=r3_iRRPakto

Nancy. (2021, May 26). *How to choose the best Instagram profile type for you.* Meet Edgar. https://meetedgar.com/blog/instagram-business-account-whats-the-difference/#:~:text=A%20basic%20account%20lets%20you

ROI Hacks Social Media Marketing Tutorials. (2022, January 22). *How to switch to an Instagram business account? [in 2022].* Www.youtube.com. https://www.youtube.com/watch?v=P367QCdlITk

SendPulse. (2022, June 22). *What is Instagram marketing: Guide - Definition.* SendPulse. https://sendpulse.com/support/glossary/instagram-marketing#:~:text=Instagram%20marketing%20is%20a%20type

Warren, J. (2021, November 19). *8 New ways to get more Instagram followers in 2019.* Later Blog. https://later.com/blog/get-more-instagram-followers/

Printed in Great Britain
by Amazon